11.95

1020 DAWSON
THORNTON, CO

PowerKids Readers:

Bilingual Edition
My Library of Holidays™
Edición Bilingüe

Gillian Houghton
Traducción al español:
Tomás González

The Rosen Publishing Group's
PowerKids Press™ & **Editorial Buenas Letras**™
New York

1

Published in 2004 by The Rosen Publishing Group, Inc.
29 East 21st Street, New York, NY 10010

First Edition

Book Design: Michael J. Caroleo

Photo Credits: Cover and pp. 13, 22 (rabbit) © Lynn Stone/ Index Stock Imagery, Inc.; pp. 5, 22 (church) © AFP/CORBIS; p. 7 © Francis G. Mayer/CORBIS; p. 9 © Bill Bachmann/ Index Stock Imagery, Inc.; p. 11 © SuperStock; p. 15 © Ariel Skelley/CORBIS; pp. 17, 22 (basket) © Eric Kamp/ Index Stock Imagery, Inc.; pp. 19, 22 (jelly beans) © Digital Stock; pp. 21, 22 (Easter lily) © Laura Hinshaw/ Index Stock Imagery, Inc.

Houghton, Gillian
Easter = Pascua / Gillian Houghton ; translated by Tomás González.
p. cm. — (My library of holidays)
Includes bibliographical references and index.
Summary: This book introduces Easter, the Christian holiday celebrating the resurrection of Jesus.
ISBN 1-4042-7526-6 (lib.)
1. Easter—Juvenile literature   [1. Easter 2. Holidays   3. Spanish language materials—Bilingual]
I. Title   II. Title: Pascua   III. Series
2004   2003-009801
394.2667—dc21

Manufactured in the United States of America

2

Contents

Contenido

Easter is a Christian holiday. Christians are people who follow the teachings of Jesus. Easter services are held in a church.

La Pascua es una fiesta cristiana. Los cristianos son personas que siguen las enseñanzas de Jesús. Los ritos de Pascua se celebran en una iglesia.

About 2,000 years ago, Jesus was killed. Christians believe that Jesus came back to life three days after his death. Easter honors this day each spring.

Hace unos 2,000 años mataron a Jesús. Los cristianos creen que Jesús resucitó tres días después de su muerte. La Pascua celebra ese acontecimiento cada primavera.

Easter is a good day. I wear my best clothes to church.

La Pascua es un buen día. Me pongo mi mejor ropa para ir a la iglesia.

9

We color the shells of eggs. The egg is a sign of new life.

Pintamos huevos con colores. El huevo es símbolo de vida nueva.

11

The rabbit is a sign of birth. Children look forward to the coming of the Easter bunny.

El conejo es símbolo de nacimiento. Los niños esperan con ilusión la llegada del conejo de Pascua.

In many families, the adults hide brightly colored eggs, and the children search for them.

En muchas familias, los adultos esconden huevos pintados con colores vivos para que los niños los busquen.

Many children receive a basket of candy on Easter morning.

Muchos niños reciben una canasta de dulces la mañana de Pascua.

Jelly beans are an Easter candy. They are shaped like small eggs.

Los dulces de goma en forma de pequeños huevos son una de las golosinas de la Pascua.

The white Easter lily is a sign of goodness, hope, and birth. The lily helps Christians remember the wonder of Jesus' return to life.

El lirio blanco de la Pascua es símbolo de bondad, esperanza y vida. El lirio ayuda a los cristianos a recordar la maravilla del regreso de Jesús a la vida.

21

Words to Know
Palabras que debes saber

basket
canasta

church
iglesia

Easter lily
lirio de Pascua

jelly beans
dulces en
forma de
huevos

rabbit
conejo

22

Here are more books to read about Easter/
Otros libros que puedes leer sobre la Pascua:

In English/En inglés:

Whole Family
by Jill O'Connor
Chronicle Books

The Easter Story
by Brian Wildsmith
Eerdmans Books for Young Readers

In Spanish/En español:

Huevos de Pascua
by Francisco Segovia
Fondo de Cultura Económica

Due to the changing nature of Internet links, PowerKids Press has developed an online list of Web sites related to the subject of this book. This site is updated regularly. Please use this link to access the list:

http://www.buenasletraslinks.com/hol/pas

Index

Índice

Words in English: 151   Palabras en español: 170

Note to Parents, Teachers, and Librarians

PowerKids Readers books *en español* are specially designed for emergent Hispanic readers and students learning Spanish in the United States. Simple stories and concepts are paired with photographs of real kids in real-life situations. Sentences are short and simple, employing a basic vocabulary of sight words, as well as new words that describe familiar things and places. With their engaging stories and vivid photo-illustrations, PowerKids *en español* gives children the opportunity to develop a love of reading and learning that they will carry with them throughout their lives.